Love is Sensational:
Figments of Emotions and Imagination

Tristen Goodwin

Copyright © 2018 by Tristen Goodwin

Cover Design: Done by Tristen Goodwin Copyright © Canva 2018

All rights reserved. This book or any portion thereof may not be reproduced or used in any manner whatsoever without the express written permission of the publisher except for the use of brief quotations in a book review or scholarly journal.

First Printing: 2018

ISBN: 978-0-578-20665-3

www.tristengoodwin.com

Ordering Information:

Special discounts are available on quantity purchases by corporations, associations, educators, and others. For details, contact the publisher at the above listed address.

U.S. trade bookstores and wholesalers: Please contact Tristen Goodwin Tel: (917)504-4775 or email tristen.writer@gmail.com

Contents

Acknowledgements iv
Preface vii
Perhaps This is What They Call Awakening 3
This Side 6
If It Was the Other Way Around 9
I May Know, But Do I Really Understand? 12
Regret 15
Desires Is What Gave Birth to Me 18
Passion 20
Student-Teacher 22
Open Letter to Myself 24
Letting Go of My Burdens 28
Happiness 31
How does that make you feel? 32
Relationships 34
Connectivity 35
A New Ending and Beginning 36
Catalyst: 37
Three golden birds: 38
Love is Sensational 41
About the Author 42

Acknowledgements

This book is a culmination of all my experiences as a living being. It was a journey displaying who I used to be and who I currently am. I hold so much gratitude for the people that surround me currently as well as those who were with me previously in my journey. My friends, family, professors, and mentors, whether they realized it or not, have allowed this co-creation to exist. It's all thanks to the experiences that were brought to me regardless of the good or the bad...

But if I must list them, I would have to start with the Peace Poets. Specifically, Enmanuel for inspiring me to work on this project, but also the group due to the work you guys do all around the world. Frantz, you inspired me with the understanding that being a nerd is one of the most powerful things that you can do to honor your identity in this world alongside Lorisse. Abraham, you really taught me through your artistry and advice, as those things empowered me as a writer and a poet. Frankie, you have always been cool and calming to talk to; and we always see eye to eye so thank you for your support. Luke, you always have the people's interest in mind through your words and actions, and always gave me a reminder about everyone's intrinsic worth. Thank you all for your mentorship.

I also have to thank the staff members and friends at The BrotherHood-Sister Sol, who have raised me into the person I currently am. Living across the street from this organization makes me quite honored and privileged in more ways than one. Whether it is just seeing you guys in the neighborhood due to some occurrence or suddenly being put to work in the brownstone is such a fun experience. This was the entry point to which my life has changed for the better, and it is what I considered my third home/family. I got to meet and interact with so many of you throughout these six years. The interactions I had with you all have raised me and given me strength.

Thank you to David Williams and Katie Cercone, as my most recent mentors, for all your insights on how to be an artist! You two helped me expand upon my spirituality, and I am deeply grateful for the work that we done together!

My friends, I'm pretty sure most of you didn't know I was writing this book at all. For those who did know, I hold so much gratitude for your support! The thanks are for all the moments that I shared with you no matter how short or how long. You have taught me something throughout time. There are so many of you that I honor and love dearly, because of these interactions. Every single one of you are a reason why this book is a co-creation. To those friends that pre-ordered the book while I was going through the complications of making it, thank you!!!

To my parents, Anthony Goodwin and Sandra Hilton, I owe you my sincere thanks for blessing me into this world, and raising me to be the person that I am. While one of you have transitioned from this world, the time that we had with each other is what brought me to this point. I owe both of you more thanks than ever before, but Mom, thank you for taking on a role that is filled with so much difficulty and hardship. Thank you for the happy moments and the moments of difficulty because without both, we wouldn't have the relationship we have now, would we? This book is a symbol of all that we been through.

My brother, Jason Davis, you brought me into the world of "nerd-ism", and that is enough to say thanks. It was due to your personal battles that reminded me of how strong every person can be. No matter the difficulties, you continue moving, and that is inspiring. Our conversations have just as much impact onto the creation of this book, and that is something in which I say thank you.

To my sister, Konya Goodwin, thank you for reuniting with me for all these years. You have been so supportive since the minute we reunited with each other. Thank you for being supportive of my endeavors, no matter how crazy they may be!!

To my teachers and professors, who exchanged with me more than lessons in the classroom, thank you for your guidance in everything. The conversations invoked in our meetings grounded me more times than I could count.

To the people that came before me including my living elders, thank you for instilling in me how powerful we are. Let this book be a message in your honor.

And to the people reading this book, thank you so much for supporting my first self-published book!! I can't express the amount of humility and appreciation I feel, but I am sincerely grateful!

Preface

Thank you so much for taking the time to read *Love is Sensational: Figments of Emotions and Imagination!* This book is a three-year project where I was inspired to take the emotions that I felt every month and combine them with imaginative fiction. Every story is a moment that felt real, as they hold an experience in each paragraph, grounding the human experience that I hold and honor. When editing, I noticed that these stories at first was no longer in alignment of who I currently am. These stories no longer reflect the way that I think and perceive feelings, so, I was inspired to add more content to allow myself to ground the lessons that I hold to the core of my being. Let this not reflect your life experiences for all of you have many different and beautiful experiences, but let it be a way for me to connect with you and share the lessons in which I learned.

One of my mentors, Enmanuel, felt that I should create a poetry chapbook a few years ago which gave inspiration to this. It was something that I personally felt odd about given how I felt about my writing at the time, being intimate and personal. During the summer of 2015, I decided that instead of the book focusing on poetry, that it could have a bunch of short stories. This book is a gateway to my thoughts, feelings, and the way I interact with the world. The title suggests an idea that love can be seen in any situation, no matter what. This means to see circumstances in ways that are meant to serve you, not to see them as things that are against you. Let this book be an intimate conversation between me and you. Let love be a sensational experience!

All love,

Tristen Goodwin
June 2018

The divinity that I create through our sacred bond is a sign that all can be sacred. No longer is it about relegating tasks to each other but embodying the sacred truth we be as we live on a matriarch that holds us. We are beautiful and perfect so there's no reason to go against that. Recognizing that all is simple is the fact that we are guided to become our higher selves and to enjoy the experiences we been given as those are sacred. I, with intention, co-create this passage for all as an affirmation to our wholeness. We are never weak, but so magically powerful that we can make choices that shift realities.

Freedom leads to choice; awakening into that understanding is what allow our lives to truly shine...

Perhaps This is What They Call Awakening

…Feeling unsure about myself, I leave behind the things that I used to consider important. I want to change for either the better or the worse, but this unhealthy desire comes from within, seeping throughout my veins. I don't know what allowed me to be consumed by such feelings, but I no longer feel like I'm on the road towards inner peace. I feel the chaotic nature within my life, and it frightens me so. I feel the uncompassionate virtue of individualism leading me down an abyss. It's not for anyone to understand, it's not for me to understand. But I understand that this desire comes from a past self that was encaged long ago. I don't want to remember the suffering I underwent long ago, but regardless I now recognize the fact that the past is what molded me. It is what held me as my support and as such continues to fuel me with this negative energy. I won't change for the better; there is no point in doing so anyway. I made my decision to let go of my pleasant life; it's to meet reality in actual flesh. It's to meet the instinctual lifestyle that man had to face before the structure called civilization began. I have accepted my fate as a slave of my instinct. This isn't the first time… My life is in my hands, and there are beings out here that are sent to get it with no care in the world. In a sense, I wouldn't have it any other way. My life always wanted to be a part of the unruly danger.

Feathers put me to rest, allowing sleep to flow through the body into the soul; unconsciousness is awake but we are asleep. I call to the heavens to see if freedom is existence, but I can't find the way there in the same way of how birds soar through the world. Like how the water flows in a river regardless of the stationary obstacles in front of it, to how the earth either shakes or bring foundation, or even the wind gently bringing a cool breeze or strong gust in its being. The nature that we are a part of, may be aware of itself but are we aware of ourselves? Perhaps this is what they call Awakening, something that is far more unnoticed then you would expect. This is the fire that lights our passions and will. To recognize the strength that flows through you, from the cells to the body, and ultimately recognizing the blood that flows within the world. We are the world…

To choose one thing or the other is a choice, but which one leads to the sensations and understandings of freedom?

This Side

We think thoughts are a common mill of the day occurrence, but perspective leads to interloping truths that brings things to the surface. The wind could gently blow the windmill forward but could also blow it viciously into acceleration; if our mind works the same way, what would be the wind? We have to be gentle with ourselves to understand that our thoughts show us what we feel and how we can always change the trajectories of what we think. Thinking is a habit, so one step at a time, where you can move to a different side of the spectrum. You can reach for joy, excitement, or peace but also for a perpetuation of the opposite. What side you belong at, is only up to you…

If I received everything I wanted from the time I was a kid to now, I would be miserable. The convoluted feeling that would be contained inside me would break me like glass. I'm glad that I'm broken not from my desires, but my experiences. That means that external forces already attacked my internal system… My mind is what contains the strength that bonds my will and knowledge together. I am what I see myself as but am I what I say I am? This question is the true definition of myself as it is the confusion that has amassed within me since I was thirteen. As this world continues to revolve around the chaos that it is victim to, I am revolving around the amassed confusion of my life. This side of my psyche is only the beginning, as my feelings love to seek the darkness of the unknown, and when I want to present them into the light... They just fade away, leaving a vessel of incompletion that fake emotions. Isn't it funny that I could articulate this with such details that make me seem real? If only people knew what they really were, the world and I wouldn't be in such chaos. Maybe it's actually the other way around...

The trajectories that life has, the ones that we see and don't see, can we appreciate the perfection of it all?

If It Was the Other Way Around

I feel the continuous amount of sadness that sends me shivers throughout my body. Understanding that fate is what leads me here as one individual, but also knowing that if fate made even a 1-degree angle in any direction, my life would be different. It saddens me that at any point, I could have ended up as a different person. There isn't any luck included in this, but the universe's dictation in my life has made me realize that my actions, thoughts, and feelings will always affect others regardless of intention. It's like I'm a ticking bomb ready to explode, only to damage those that surround themselves around me. All the decisions that I made was for me and only me. The idea of solitude perpetuated itself, making me seem like I was the only light in the tunnel. My selfishness only led me onto a path of pain and regret. The things I need to learn will never get through to my soul because I will never feel ready to accept these lessons. If only it was the other way around, then maybe this sadness would leave my core. But perhaps I'm already in class learning the things that I need to know…

Knowledge of all things may just be knowledge of yourself, for we are everything and nothing…We tend to think the destruction of the world is controlling our path in life, but what if we chose to control our own path in life regardless of the destruction we have constant discourse over? Resistance to injustice is necessary not only on the outside but the inside, however creation is also necessary to implement the new foundations for how we want to live. But the question is, what is the priority in this case? Do you choose the world because you are a part of the world or do you choose yourself? To heal everything around you, you must heal yourself just like how a farmer feeds themselves before all else. You must provide the food for your needs so you can provide nourishment to all that surrounds you.

Our will to learn is what helps us expand and understand our truth bit by bit, slowly or rapidly...

I May Know, But Do I Really Understand?

Seeking a place in the world is a noble cause… You look around on a giant piece of life, a place that could eventually give you a reason to be content with yourself. However, time steadily walks toward you, showing you how the amazing trait of your species can also reflect their disgusting negativity. Should I feel proud that I am part of the human race, where we are a collective that is trying to acquire a place individually? When did this feeling even arrive, I continue to think as I drag myself through the booming and crowded streets. Where everyone that I refuse to acknowledge appear as shadowy figures creeping in any direction. Perhaps social norms and monetary distribution contributed to this race and myself, but why do I feel rejected from the place I was born in. I know that life will always go on like a friend moving away, but what can I do if I feel comfortable in this abstract space of mine. Solitude will never leave me, which I got to say is an ironic twist since it was never a friend. In a way, I love the black and white world I created for myself…no one will never be able to know me, the real me… I never once felt contempt with my life, but do I understand what life really is? If only the answer was given to me would I have such a conundrum? Who knows…?

Knowledge is more than memorization, knowledge is the journey towards the unknown where mistakes are made. Knowledge is an active part of being human, and integrating it is quite passive. Similar to how fishes following the flow of the currents at the right place and time, we must allow ourselves to gain knowledge that help form our own understandings about ourselves on a physical, mental, and emotion/spiritual level. We must constantly challenge ourselves to get to the place we want to be, for that is the remembrance of what power is. Empowerment is an inner knowing of worth but it's also the understanding of where you fit, no matter what occurs. The journey of a seer is not one without challenges but one where every challenge is nothing more but an experience of humility and learning. We are all seers regardless if we identify as such for we all hold important knowledge that can help create newness.

To be deep in the shadow of regret is to be human, but don't allow regret to dictate your fate for only you can define your fate...

Regret

Regret is a cool thing in my eyes. You think about past experiences, and BOOM; you've been hit with guilt and the feeling of pitying yourself. I guess you guys can tell I'm in a bad mood, I feel burdened by many things like not having the ability to completely analyze my life and deleting all these temporary memories in my brain. Man, I'm not in a good mood..., quietly I wish how I could just spend time on a rooftop in solitude. I regret not feeling the cool breeze and stargazing that one star that wasn't blocked by pollution. I like solitude...; it gave me the ability to think about things and it has gotten me out of trouble. But I regret not spending time with them...This is another story for another time. Every time I wish to speak my mind, I just can't. My level of expression is pretty low, since I never put the time into raising my stats. My gaming skills are slowly declining, and perhaps that speak volumes. I guess you could say that I fucked myself over so many times, that my current mood defines the word fragmented. Regret leaves me fragmented, only giving me desires to combine again…

Our wants are just as necessary as our needs, the world may dictate what you should do, but your wants are what make you powerful. We regret when something doesn't happen when expected, but that is what expectations mostly create. We may expect all practicality and logic to serve us at every point, but what happens when it doesn't? How do we deal with the identity of expectations and what are we putting expectations on? How does regret play with the idea of expectations and how do we burden ourselves so? We can regret nothing when we are following the path that brings us joy because that is what our truth represents.

Our wants, the dreams that are a part of us just as much as our needs are...when we honor our desires then what are we truly doing?

Desires Is What Gave Birth to Me

Desire is what led humans to follow sheer emotion more so than logical progression, and perhaps that is the main factor that gave form to the world we currently live in today. The desires I am thinking about may portray all the negative corresponding ideas that many think of. I mean lust, greed, and gluttony all gave birth to several human beings that we consistently give critique and perhaps ruin to. I mean it gave birth to me; Remember that a child requires nourishment and nothing from this world comes free, well supposedly. But personally, my desires are neither malignant or benevolent. To be quite honest, I don't know what I really want, and that's why I'm constantly lost in this imaginary forest I made for myself. The knowledge I took from so many, and you would think I would have a clear-cut path for myself. Nope; it's more like this bullshit just driven me back three steps because "surprisingly" not every human is treated equally. I think what I truly desire is to explain my thought process and see where I can go with many people. The difference that I see in each person is what gave birth to my desire which internally gave birth to me. Unfortunately love and lust only go so far with me, since those desires are just buried away, and even greed have no place in my heart because I love my life currently and ironically. I learned to appreciate the subtler things as life go onwards, but then again, I'm just a college student…

A student that was learning, is now mastering his ideas and his desires. We have been humbled by this world as many feel it is wrong to follow their aspirations, but instead this is what co-creation leads to. Desires are always co-creations when you really look at it, regardless of intentions, regardless of morality. Our desires are just as sacred as we are, as nothing is ever absolute in the world, but our infinite worth and the concept of change. As we continue to work towards our desires, we are honestly going through evolution, learning more about ourselves and where we fit in the world. When we desire the world to be a better place, could this also be a desire for us to be a better person? What does the world outside of you mean in relation to the world inside of you? Who do you want to be in this world? When we want to become a better person or see the traits that we want to possess, doesn't that mean you already became that version of yourself? For all desires lead us through, a period of death and rebirth...

Passion

Calls out to me like a bell

Takes me to point A to point B

Never letting me stop

So I can reach new heights

The lengths it takes to keep me in track

Is solemnity in abstract form

Is my words in tangibility

Is my love in actuality

Is my emotions in actions

Passion calls out to me like God's calls

To help this world

To see myself

And to see you

As the mass of love you always been...

I see the reflection of me within your eyes, showing me the light in all that I am as I do for you...

Student-Teacher

It's been a while since I last jotted down my imaginative and emotional experiences. However, I learned that these feelings, regardless if I determined them as false, are all real. Everything that I last spoke about, portrayed myself as a contradicting enigma, but perhaps I'm okay with that. It's hard to accept the many bad endings that life provides you, but when you come to see the light at the ending of that play and all the actors bowing down, it becomes beautiful. My life, I learned, is beautiful where the bad endings and the failures play a role just as much as the happy beginnings and accomplishments. I mean I still play a cynical role in many people's lives because it's entertaining, but I hope they all understand that they mean a lot more to me than I show. My emotions are showing and I'm been called sensitive many times, but I guess it presents the fact that at my weakest point, this is who I truly am. I'm glad that I found this new facet of myself because I learned so much, but there is so much more to do. The tutorial that life gives you is nonexistent but that's because we don't need one. I come to realize that life is destined but at the same time not destined. We're able to define our lives as many times as we want before our end, but with each choice we make, life now makes a path for us. I don't know if you understand, but currently that's how I accepted my life to be. My current dream is to surpass my present self. In anything…because I have so much more to teach myself. But perhaps I need to learn that my dreams may have already become realities.

Open Letter to Myself

Living life lustfully with congruent intentions of being lively

Happiness seem so far away when you feel trapped inside

Ego is consuming

Desires are corrupting

Dreams are decaying

Don't even let me bring up hopes...

Everything seem hopeful

From the empty promises or the fake smiles

Leading a life of deceit seem easy

Emotions are a foreign language

Knowledge is a common problem

Consequences means nothing

Theory of higher consciousness surrounds you

Leading you to something more

Grasping whatever you can get

Regardless of authenticity

It's seems to be real

It's real enough to cause pain

Misery never seem so real

This is the truth so far

But I been lying midway

Coping with yourself is hard enough

When love is nothing to you but to be vulnerable

Creating cracks on the statue of perfection

you encased yourself in

is scary

Evoking the narcissism in me

Is pretty easy

Good deeds and Good will lead to apparent acceptance

But is that flowing with

the river that was set in my heart

Wasting life for the sense of purpose

seem normal in this world

Why not continue the pattern?

Revival of self is ongoing

The truth was set in the past but has led me here

Witness the road I make

Regardless of the errors

Regardless of the hatred

Renewal for that sense of love, you always wanted

From,

"The guy who does mystical shit"

As a journeyer of this world, we have to carry a necessary amount of weight but we are never obligated to carry what is not ours...

Letting Go of My Burdens

I started to accept myself as time continue onwards. It was a liberating experience I must say as I'm in a dark place currently but I gained happiness anyway. I more or less moved on from my suffering, and talking to people made me realize what I'm like. I'm leaving my burdens one by one as I continue on this journey. It's an amazing phenomenon, just like how the world rotates through the seasons, it feels like I'm on a continuous spring cleaning job. Ha-ha, A joke that's corny, but I'm powerless against the ongoing waves of emotions that are inside me. You never did anything to hurt me, it was just a transition in emotions. Perhaps that's what hurt, because I thought we could be together through any struggle, but this shows otherwise. I'm sorry that my vulnerability is showing, but I love you and I will continue to, no matter what. If life presents fortuitous events for us to collide once again, we will work for our happiness separately or together. This, used-to-be hopeless romantic, believes there is still a chance, but I will never hold you back as that would be holding myself back. It's really the heartbeats that echo in my being every minute that allows these feelings to come out, but the time that we spent with each other, while short, was beautiful. I can let go because tomorrow is a new day and I'm happy that I received such a great experience from the point we met to when we started a new beginning. This is a beginning of my burdens becoming my pillars towards greatness…for our burdens grants us a chance to create a new foundation for life to begin anew.

We often hold ourselves to things that we can't always control. Letting go of your burdens is letting go of the need to control, for there is nothing that truly needs to be controlled. If the burdens you hold is consuming you and not uplifting you, what does that tell you? Sometimes, burdens seem intergenerational, but as long as one person takes the weight off, there is clearance and peace that can surface throughout generations. I am never obligated to carry others' weight, but I have the choice to do so. We are all a part of this life together, and to continue the chain of inspiration, I know I have the strength to carry my brother's or sister's burdens. An empowered individual within a collective, what are the results of such a fusion? As one let go of their burdens, does that create ripple effects for others?

The power we feel, share, exchange, honor, and express is the beacon of what we all are, I am free because I choose to be, just so I can allow myself to express...

Happiness

Joy is the thing that could be seen as far away or close by. Maybe because I have no thoughts on this subject; I can't find any words to oppose or impose on the happiness of others. I have sworn against the impurities of the world and decided to remove most of my humanity. (So, I think...) My happiness...is continuously organized in a random manner letting it be seen throughout the external eyes of the world, but all the while I'm grasping true actuality of the feeling. I question if I am worthy of such a valuable part of the soul and I realized that everyone is. In a field full of flowers, I realized a flower's serenity is not because of their fate but the reflection of what we bear witness to. We who are composed of Earth's ever-present bounty, have the same potential to reach the state of a flower. Happiness surrounds us when all that is temporary is released, and let the reminder be that happiness is everything.

How does that make you feel?

When thoughts proceeding to weigh you down to hell

Knowing they aren't reality but scared they could be

It's a process to learn

But just let go

And surpass your current self

But remember to love throughout the process...

Because that's all you are at the end of time

My consciousness is up here while my passions are down here

Emotions lending dualistic personalities showing love and hate

But don't hate me now when I'm at my weakest

I'm just letting go of my weakness

When I find myself, I'll show you how I feel

When the time is right

When my world is back

There's nothing to hold me back

As long as I got you and me

Now let me ask you "How does that make you feel?"

I honor the exchange we made even if I never met you in the physical world, but interconnectedness is a reality that we coexist in, but what happens if we co-create together? These stories are a thread that cannot be cut for true power is within us all.

Relationships

I wanderlust the sea of consciousness trying to reach my higher self. Through the people that I meet like broken stairs coming together leading my subconscious. It's all to give a helping hand when someone reaches this point…but empty promises hit me like bricks bringing me closer to my earthly despair. But water is cleansing as my soul is a river that will flow in the right direction. My being is taken with discretion but hopefully someone along the way try to challenge all that I am…. but…there's no need. I need no individual to challenge myself but me as I am the stake that hold the chains of my bonds. As I am the foundation toward my relations with others. As I am part of the world everlasting, creating new experiences in a whole body. I am not incomplete, nor will I ever be incomplete. This sea of consciousness is not the place to die, but our place to prosper… But I'm so closed off as my heart can't be found, not by me or anyone else. Scared of betrayal or rejection, I hid my truest form in the dark. I don't need someone to challenge my being, but I need to find my heart so I can challenge everything.

Connectivity

Smelling the freshness in air, releasing the fear and anxiety as carbon dioxide but receiving peace as oxygen

Touch and sound intermix having handshakes give impacts leading to sonic booms breaking disconnection

Sight is seeing your reflection from another's eye watching the hope you gave reflected at you...

Taste is the traditions that years cultivated throughout time lending a story each time you enjoy the earth's bounty

Sense is the feeling of belonging knowing the energy you send is added in union making interconnections within easy

Transitioning in constant change is only natural as water flows, trees grow and die, wind blows gently or forcefully, and fire burns or dies...

A New Ending and Beginning

It been a battlefield for a while now, where my thoughts and feelings often fought for hours to days to even months. Now everything is destroyed, barren…I think nothingness is approaching as death besieges me. Though there is one thing that decided to leave its presence, in this vast battlefield shining in a light I never gazed upon. A stem showing potential for growth, a foreseen actuality that life can come again where peace brings itself through the wind to the water. I crawled to the only sign of life to only tremble in disbelief and relinquish all sadness. What have I been fighting for and why did I go through this would be the questions that I asked in complete rage, but honestly, I was with complete silence.

I knew why this needed to happen and what I was fighting for. The struggle to survive so I can change for the better was a goal that I felt wouldn't require such trials…how wrong I was. There's a chance for me to become this beacon of life, hope. Letting go of my burdens was only one of the difficulties, and relationships led me here. I realized now that this battle was more for me than I thought. This unruly danger has certainly taken me in this direction, but now I understand that this war was my awakening. I now understand what being authentic is and the fact that I needed to be catalyzed to begin anew.

Catalyst:

I breathe the air inside me as I feel discord internally. My awakening was based off fear and hate, but now I see beauty in all things. I understand my place, my belonging… I was catalyzed to find a calling unlike any other. My true awakening occurred way before my initial "AWAKENING". Truth can be taken in a subjective manner but at the same time it isn't subjective at all. I'm more than just an object of the world and so are you. Imagine a forest with leaves that hold a multitude of colors. Colors are infinite in nature, why do you think when they're transmuted together you get the color white to symbolize the harmony. We're all leaves that are part of the tree called growth as our roots belong to this planet. Showing our connectivity to our home, each other, and ourselves. History is just an accumulation of the experiences within us all in the present. And our tree represents this, but we're more than that, for we're catalysts for the world's growth.

Three golden birds:

Senseless imagery showed three golden birds flying in a circle looking to combine; I can't find ways to express what this means but by finding methods to fly out of my cage. I noticed birds represent freedom and I don't mean the American eagle but many of them have the choice to fly. A choice is something that we often surmise as something feeble but never treat it as the power it's known to have. To have choice denotes freedom which ultimately defines love. Now love is limitless like we all "know", but the question is: have we really reached the echelon of what love really is? Birds flying is similar to love because it's natural, it's a choice. We're free to change at any point, at any day, at any moment growing and reaching new heights as spiritual beings in a physical form.

I ask you if you want to love, and no, I don't mean conditional love where you egotistically close your heart in search of expectations. Love is the idea of being comfortable and authentic with yourself, to the point that you reveal your truth every moment no matter the judgement. I ask do you want to fly like those birds who have those choices, becoming a being of authenticity and love? Where you live your joy at every moment you have. Three golden birds are the imagery I've seen to encompass this advice, to just tell you to follow your joy without judgement. Every judgement you receive has nothing to do with you but everyone who judge and if it gets to you then rise from it. Let everything that you encounter become a teacher where you become grateful for your "enemies" and your allies. The sky isn't the limit because growth is everlasting even till our last breath so spread your wings and fly the path you were meant to soar. I say this as a fellow person who sees his reflection in all of you.

These stories, the words that lead you to the epicenter of all that I hold sacred, as this is my magnus opus…

Love is Sensational

To the self

With the friends and the lover

Letting my darkness be embraced

Opposing the negativity, it brings

Virtuously it's amazing and

Everything it holds is a blessing

Love. is. sensational

Innately supreme

Solely Profound

Sensations are everywhere

Never are there singular aspirations

Tainting my internal origin

All or Nothing

is what life is

Because

Love is Sensational...

Let it surround you with union

About the Author

Tristen Anthony Goodwin was born in New York City where he was raised in the Bronx and is currently living in Harlem.

He started writing poetry at the end of high school. His works were inspired by the things that surrounded him, which were video games and graphic novels. The stories within those mediums gave him his love of philosophy and his introspectiveness that allowed his words to take on those elements. His works, comes from the belief that all can be empowered, by looking at situations, people, and surroundings in ways that allow us to grow. Tristen is a graduate of Manhattan College and is currently enrolled at the CUNY Graduate Center.

Furthermore, he is also a tarot card reader, using the skill to break down the idea of fortune telling by promoting the message that "we control fate". His readings promote the idea that at any moment, we can always be our highest selves. This practice has expanded his understandings of who we are as a collective and as individuals.

He is the creator of his web page: www.tristengoodwin.com where he currently posts his own writings and host his tarot card services.

For more info on the author visit:
www.tristengoodwin.com

Find him on:
Instagram: t_for_tarot10
Email: tristen.writer@gmail.com

www.ingramcontent.com/pod-product-compliance
Lightning Source LLC
Chambersburg PA
CBHW031436040426
42444CB00006B/838